"Centi" means a hundred and "milli" means a thousand, but despite their names, centipedes and millpedes do not have hundreds or thousands of legs. They just look like they do. There are, however, thousands of differents sorts of them.

Both are invertebrates, meaning that they have no backbone. Instead they have an exoskeleton, a hard outer skin that covers their insides.

Centipedes' bodies are divided into parts called segments. Each segment has one pair of legs on it. Centipedes always have an odd number of pairs of legs. From the head end, each pair of legs is a bit longer on each segment. This helps them to walk without getting their legs tangled up.

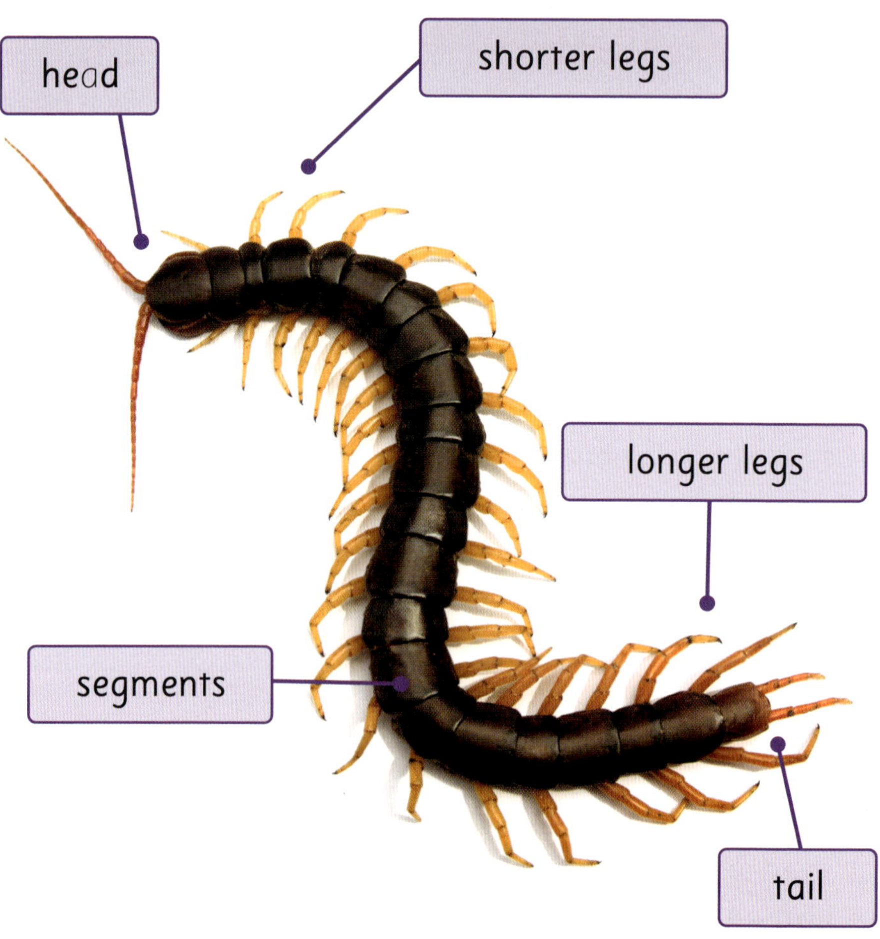

Centipedes have a flat head with an antenna on each side of the head. They cannot see very well and use these to find things to eat.

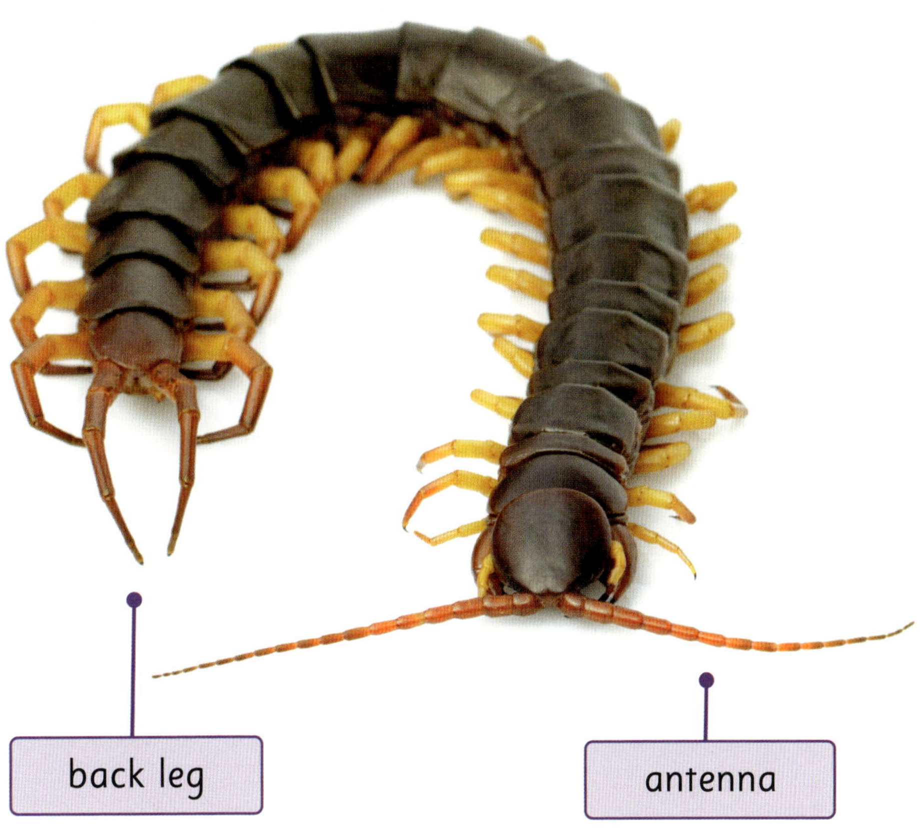

They also have a long pair of legs at the back. A back leg looks like an antenna. This makes it difficult to know which is the head end and which is the tail end when you look at them.

Centipedes live in many different places – in gardens, in woodland, on the seashore, in sheds, and in houses. They also live in tropical rainforests and deserts, and even in the Arctic circle. They need a moist place to live and so are often found in soil, under stones, and dead wood, and inside old logs.

Centipedes eat other insects and animals. When they sense a spider, a slug, or a smaller insect such as a fly, they chase after it and pounce on it. They use their pincers to hold the animal down and inject poison. Centipedes can run very quickly.

Millipedes look similar to centipedes but they are in fact quite different. Millipedes have two pairs of legs on each body segment.

A centipede's legs stick out at the side of the body, whereas a millipede's legs go down. Millipedes eat decaying (rotting) leaves and other vegetable matter.

If threatened, millipedes coil up to protect their soft underbellies and their heads, while centipedes quickly scuttle away and hide. Millipedes spend a lot of time underground, burrowing in the soil or under stones to keep under cover and out of sight.

a millipede coiled up

Millipedes and centipedes are eaten by many other animals, such as birds, badgers, frogs, and toads.

Some centipedes have a defense mechanism, however. If they are being held by an animal that is trying to eat them, they can drop the legs being held and then run away on the rest of their legs.

Most centipedes lay eggs in spaces in the soil. When they hatch, the young look similar to the adults, but they might not have any legs. As they get bigger, they split their external skins and grow more segments and legs.

Some types of centipedes can live for five to six years.

Common centipedes (also known as brown or stone centipedes) have long, thin, brownish-red bodies. They are found under the cover of stones or bark, and in soil or decaying matter.

They normally have 18 (eighteen) segments and 15 (fifteen) pairs of legs. They use their long back legs as feelers so that they can walk backwards almost as quickly as forwards.

Common centipedes do not see very well, so they feel their way around and are most active at night. They are an aggressive predator. They chase after and eat lots of garden insects and pests, so they can be a gardener's friend.

They lay single eggs in the soil. A common centipede can live for about three years.

Amazonian giant centipedes are the largest type. They have been known to eat lizards, frogs, birds, mice, bats, snakes, and spiders, including tarantulas.

They can climb to the top of caves to catch bats. They have yellow legs and are 10 inches (30cm) long. They prefer to live and hunt alone.

Most common millipedes have about 34 - 400 (thirty-four to four hundred) legs, not a thousand!

giant African millipede

The giant African millipede is the largest sort of millipede. It can grow up to 13.2 inches long (33.5cm) and have 30 to 50 (thirty to fifty) body segments. It lives mostly on the ground in the forests of East Africa, and it feeds on decaying matter.

One sort of millipede found in California, in the United States of America, is tiny at only 0.4 - 1.2 inches long (1 to 3cm), but it can have as many as 750 (seven hundred and fifty) legs. They live under sandstone rocks, and their legs have evolved to be able to cling onto these rocks.

Bristly millipedes got their name because they have little hairs, called bristles, on them. They have fewer legs than other millipedes and are very small, no longer than 0.3 inches (7mm).

Bristly millipedes' hairs can come off and get tangled in the legs or mouths of other animals, such as ants, which might try to eat them.

Centipedes and millipedes are some of the oldest animals on Earth. Fossils have been found that are 400 million years old. No complete fossils have been found, but long parallel rows of small fossilized footprints have been found in many places. We think that they were originally herbivores and only ate leaves and vegetable matter.

giant millipede fossil

Some of the fossilized centipedes and millipedes found were nearly 6 feet long (2m). Imagine meeting one of those!